curiousabout

HIKING

BY ELIZABETH KASSUELKE

AMICUS LEARNING

What are you

curious about?

CHAPTER THREE

3

Getting Out There
PAGE
16

Curious About is published by Amicus Learning,
an imprint of Amicus
P.O. Box 227
Mankato, MN 56002
www.amicuspublishing.us

Editor: Alissa Thielges
Series Designer: Kathleen Petelinsek
Book Designer: Lori Bye
Photo Researcher: Omay Ayres

Library of Congress Cataloging-in-Publication Data
Names: Kassuelke, Elizabeth, author.
Title: Curious about hiking / by Elizabeth Kassuelke.
Description: Mankato, MN : Amicus, [2024] | Series: Curious
about the great outdoors | Includes bibliographical references
and index. | Audience: Ages 5–9 years | Audience: Grades 2–3
| Summary: "Questions and answers give kids the fundamentals
of hiking, including gear and safety tips. Includes infographics to
support visual learning and back matter to support research skills,
plus a glossary and index"—Provided by publisher.
Identifiers: LCCN 2023010687 (print) | LCCN 2023010688
(ebook) | ISBN 9781645496632 (library binding) | ISBN
9781681529523 (paperback) | ISBN 9781645496892 (pdf)
Subjects: LCSH: Hiking—Juvenile literature. |
Walking—Juvenile literature.
Classification: LCC GV199.52 .K37 2024 (print) |
LCC GV199.52 (ebook) | DDC 796.51—
dc23/eng/20230407
LC record available at https://lccn.loc.gov/2023010687
LC ebook record available at https://lccn.loc.gov/2023010688

Photo credits: Getty/Erik Isakson/Tetra Images, 6, FatCamera,
20, Maskot, 17, Per Breiehagen, 15, Thomas Barwick, 8, 9;
Shutterstock/Abramova Elena, 15, bixstock, 15, Blazej Lyjak,
cover, 1, Hong Vo, 15, Jacob Lund, 5, JGA, 14, minizen, 22,
Ratana Prongjai, 15, sjgh, 10, T. Schneider, 13, Warren Metcalf,
12, Yukhymets Vladyslav, 19, Zheltyshev, 13, zhukovvlad, 21

Printed in China

CHAPTER ONE

Is hiking different from just walking?

Yes. You can take a walk anywhere, even indoors. It is usually short and easy to do. Hiking is a longer trip through nature. It is always outdoors. Hikers follow a set **trail**. The paths are rougher and take more strength.

DID YOU KNOW?

Hiking was extra popular in 2020 in the United States. People couldn't gather indoors because of the COVID pandemic, so they went outside.

Hiking trails are often covered in dirt and rocks.

Can I go hiking?

The first person can set the hiking speed for the group.

Yes! Hiking is for everyone. Some trails are easy, and some are difficult. Some people hike to be the fastest. Some try to go the farthest. But most people take their time. Hiking is an easy way to get moving.

Are there rules to hiking?

Protecting nature lets people enjoy it for many years.

The golden rule of hiking is "leave no trace." Everything you bring has to come home with you. Even trash. It also means that you should stay on the trail. This protects you and the wildlife.

CHAPTER TWO

Where can I hike?

Almost anywhere! There are over 200,000 miles (321,869 kilometers) of hiking trails in the United States. Can't find a trail? Try out **urban hiking**. Walk through a city on sidewalks or trails through town. There is always somewhere to explore.

LONGEST TRAILS IN NORTH AMERICA

Trans Canada Trail

Pacific Crest Trail

Continental Divide Trail

American Discovery Trail

Appalachian Trail

GEARING UP

TRANS CANADA TRAIL:
17,398 MILES (28,000 KM)

AMERICAN DISCOVERY TRAIL:
6,800 MILES (10,944 KM)

CONTINENTAL DIVIDE TRAIL:
3,100 MILES (4,989 KM)

PACIFIC CREST TRAIL:
2,650 MILES (4,265 KM)

APPALACHIAN TRAIL:
2,180 MILES (3,508 KM)

Can hiking be dangerous?

Human voices usually scare predators away, so talk or sing while you hike.

Not usually. But there are sometimes bears and mountain lions. You can also get caught in a storm or sprain your ankle. It's best to be prepared. Bring a first aid kit and bear spray. Check the weather and read the **trailhead** map so you don't get lost. And always hike with others.

Whistle

Compass

Matches

Bear spray

First aid kit

Water bottle

DID YOU KNOW?
Some hikers carry safety gear in a backpack. They are prepared for anything.

What should I bring?

Some hikers wear hiking boots.

You don't need much. The **gear** you bring depends on the trail. Shoes with a good **tread** are a must. Grab a jacket and waterproof shoes if it's wet out. A water bottle and snacks are important, too. A camera, binoculars, and a journal can make the hike extra fun.

Good shoes keep
you steady if the trail
crosses a river.

HIKING SNACKS

granola bars

fruit

crackers

beef jerky

15

CHAPTER THREE

Will hiking get boring?

No way! Go with family or friends. You can play I-Spy or make a nature journal. You can collect rocks. Or you can take pictures of the different bugs you see. Use your imagination. Hiking is all about adventure.

Take time to stop
and look around
on your hike.

What can I see while hiking?

Keep an eye out for wildlife. Look for animal tracks, too. Squirrels and birds are common sights. Depending on where you hike, you may see deer, elk, or even bighorn sheep! Some trails lead over bridges and rivers. Others take you high up a cliff or to a cool waterfall.

A hike can lead you to beautiful natural wonders.

Why should I go hiking?

Hiking can boost your health.

Hiking is a great way to see and learn about nature. Hiking keeps your heart and muscles strong. It also builds your **endurance**. Plus, fresh air is great for you! It lowers stress and makes you happier. It helps you focus better, too.

Hiking is good exercise in the winter, too.

ASK MORE QUESTIONS

How do you train for a long hike?

Could I set a hiking record?

»——→

**Try a BIG QUESTION:
How does hiking help the Earth?**

SEARCH FOR ANSWERS

Search the library catalog or the Internet.
A librarian, teacher, or parent can help you.

Using Keywords
Find the looking glass.

🔍

Keywords are the most important words in your question.

❓

If you want to know about:

• training for a long hike, type: HIKER TRAINING

• what records to beat, type: HIKER RECORDS

FIND GOOD SOURCES

Here are some good, safe sources you can use in your research.
Your librarian can help you find more.

Books

Go Hiking! by Meghan Gottschall, 2022.

Hiking by Lisa Owings, 2023.

Hiking in Nature by Abby Colich, 2021.

Internet Sites

Hiking | Britannica Kids
https://kids.britannica.com/students/ article/hiking/274879
This encyclopedia site covers the history and basics of hiking.

Kid's Corner | American Hiking Society
https://americanhiking.org/kids/kids-corner/
This page gives information, crafts, and activities to do while hiking.

SHARE AND TAKE ACTION

Plot out a trip on nearby hiking trail.
Use a map to see how far to go and mark where to stop.

Make your own trail mix.
Mix together nuts, chocolate chips, and dried fruit and scoop the trail mix into baggies.

Make a hiking scrapbook.
Take pictures of all the places you've hiked and write a short description of the trip.

GLOSSARY

endurance The ability to do something hard for a long period of time.

gear Things needed and brought with on a hike, such as a first aid kit and water bottle.

trail A marked path through a forest or field.

trailhead A spot that marks the start of a hiking trail.

tread The thick bottom part of a shoe that grips the ground.

urban hiking Walking to explore a city.

INDEX

About the Author

Elizabeth Kassuelke is a 2023 graduate of Bethany Lutheran College in Minnesota. She loves to read, write, and spend time outside, and this book spoke to all of those passions!